OBJECT LESSONS

LESSONS

———————— Made Easy

D1456179

Also by Beth Lefgren and Jennifer Jackson:

Young Women Activities, Revised Edition

OBJECT LESSONS
—— Made Easy

BETH LEFGREN AND JENNIFER JACKSON

DESERET
BOOK

SALT LAKE CITY, UTAH

Dedicated to our families.

Thanks for teaching us, inspiring us, and supporting us.

This is a revised and updated edition of the titles previously published as *Power Tools for Teaching* and *More Power Tools for Teaching.*

Library of Congress Cataloging-in-Publication Data

Lefgren, Beth.
    Object lessons made easy : memorable ideas for gospel teaching / Beth Lefgren, Jennifer Jackson.
        p. cm.
    Includes index.
    Summary: Practical, creative object lessons arranged by subject for gospel teachers of all ages.
    ISBN 978-1-60641-899-4 (paperbound)
    1. Object-teaching. 2. Christian education—Teaching methods. I. Jackson, Jennifer. II. Title.
    BV1536.5.L4495 2010

268'.6—dc22   2010032917

Printed in the United States of America
Edwards Brothers Malloy, Ann Arbor, MI

10   9   8   7

CONTENTS

PREFACE

This book was written for you! No matter what teaching situation you find yourself in—home, church, classroom, Scouts, or community—objects are a creative way to clarify and strengthen your lessons. This helpful resource provides object lessons flexible enough to personalize, yet structured enough to be the basis of a lesson.

These teaching tools can be modified easily to fit almost any group or situation. You will discover that many activities can be quickly interchanged to meet your individual needs.

Topics are arranged alphabetically for easy location. Additionally, three valuable indexes are included in the back: one for scriptures referenced in a lesson, the second for main objects used, and the third for all lessons which could pertain to a particular subject. These indexes provide for easy reference and serve as a springboard, expanding the versatility of each object lesson.

As you use object lessons, your ability and creativity in teaching will greatly increase. You will find that your lessons will be more enthusiastic and memorable. We hope this book will contribute to your success in the most important job anyone could have—teaching.

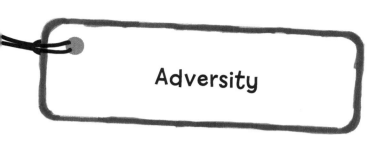

Adversity

Objective

To demonstrate that one of the purposes of adversity is to improve character.

Materials Needed

A small piece of coal and a diamond.

Procedure

Show the piece of coal. Ask what it is and what it is used for. Show the diamond, and ask what it is and how it is used.

Explain that each diamond is made of carbon, just like coal, but extreme pressure and heat transformed it into a beautiful diamond. Without so much heat and pressure, the carbon likely would have become a simple piece of coal.

Teach that Heavenly Father allows us to face adversity so that we can become better individuals. When we use trials and learning experiences to transform and enhance our character, we can become more Christlike.

Note

Although the real objects are preferred, pictures can be used effectively in their place.

Scripture References

1 Nephi 20:10; 3 Nephi 24:17.

The Coal was so plain but it improved into a Beautiful diamond.

Play Game! + Monopoly

1

Adversity

Objective

To illustrate that a strong testimony can help us handle adversity.

Materials Needed

Two paper sacks (carefully unseal part of the bottom seam of one) and three or four lemons.

Procedure

Hold up the sack with the unsealed bottom and explain that it represents a person whose testimony is not as strong as it could be. Show a lemon and explain that the lemon represents the adversity that everyone experiences in life. Drop the lemons, one by one, into the bag. The bag will fail to hold the lemons. Explain that when our testimonies are weakened, we may not be able to handle adversity as well.

Contrast this by holding up the other bag and likening it to a person with a steadfast testimony. Drop the lemons into the bag one at a time. Close the opening of the bag by folding it and then shake the bag. Explain that a strong testimony gives us inner strength and helps us cope with adversity. Even though we may be stretched and strained by the weight of the experience, we can remain strong and handle the challenge well.

Scripture References

Job 19:25–26; John 16:33.

Adversity

Objective

To show that adversity can help us become better people.

Materials Needed

A piece of rough wood, sandpaper, and a piece of newspaper to catch sawdust.

Procedure

Show the rough wood to the class and briefly discuss how it would feel. Now show and pass around the sandpaper. Ask class members to comment on how it feels. During the following discussion, rub the rough edges of the wood with the sandpaper (holding it over the newspaper). Discuss what happens as you use the sandpaper on the rough wood. Be sure to include why the sandpaper makes the wood feel smooth (rough particles cut off the rough bits of wood).

Liken the sandpaper to adversity and the wood to ourselves. Tell class members that adversity can soften and smooth our rough edges. Give some examples or ask the class to think of examples of this principle (for example, an extended illness may make a person more compassionate).

Scripture References

Doctrine and Covenants 136:31; 122:5–7.

Atonement

Objective

To help class members understand that the Atonement can help us with our burdens.

Materials Needed

A backpack and several heavy rocks.

Procedure

Ask for a class member to assist with this lesson. Show the backpack to the class and ask what it is used for. Have the volunteer put it on. Liken the backpack to our lives. Sometimes things happen in our lives and leave us with a heavy feeling. Ask: What are some things that might do this? (Examples include illness, financial problems, sin, etc.). As each item is named, put a rock into the backpack.

Point out that we sometimes allow the negative things in life to weigh us down. Ask the volunteer how the backpack feels now.

Tell the class that Heavenly Father has provided a way to ease our burden. Ask for ideas. Explain that through the Atonement, Jesus Christ can lighten the burdens of mortality.

Scripture References

Alma 7:11–12; Mosiah 24:14.

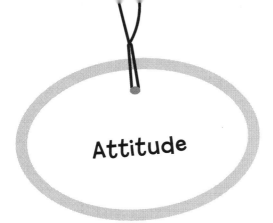

Attitude

Objective

To inspire us to have a positive attitude about life.

Materials Needed

A sheet of paper and a clear glass.

Procedure

Hold up the sheet of paper and liken it to our lives. Explain that life holds many challenges, problems, and occasionally, disappointments (for example, having a flat tire in the middle of a desert, caring for a sick relative, missing an important appointment, or losing a parent). As you name a specific problem, tear off a small piece of paper and put it in the glass.

When you are done, show the glass filled with torn paper. Explain that some people would look at these scraps of paper and say, "Look at this. My whole life has been nothing but problems." Yet others would look at the same papers, toss them in the air, and celebrate what has been overcome.

Scripture References

Mosiah 24:14–15, 21–22; Romans 8:18.

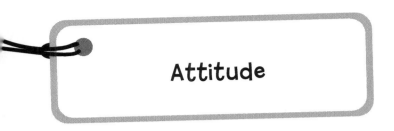

Attitude

Objective

To demonstrate that sometimes we allow small difficulties to keep us from noticing our blessings.

Materials Needed

Small pebbles and small pieces of candy.

Procedure

Give each person a pebble and a piece of candy. Instruct the class members to place the pebble in a shoe and the candy in his or her mouth. Take the class members on a short walk. (Although this works best outside, it can be adapted to a classroom situation if needed.)

After the walk, ask the group about their experience on the walk. Most will dwell on the discomfort of the pebble and say little about the good taste of the candy.

Explain that sometimes we focus on the small hardships (pebbles) that are part of life and forget the good things (candies) that are all around us. Discuss the importance of a positive attitude and how it affects us and those around us.

Scripture Reference

Job 37:14.

Avoiding
Pornography

Objective

To illustrate that contact with pornography or profanity leaves residual effects.

Materials Needed

A ripe orange and an onion.

Preparation

Slice the orange and the onion. Layer them together in a closed container for about one hour. Remove the onion and arrange the orange slices attractively on a plate for use in the lesson.

Procedure

Show the delicious-looking orange you brought for the lesson. Tell the class that you are anxious to let everyone taste it. Pass the orange slices around. Ask for comments on the taste of the orange.

Explain that the orange had only a brief encounter with the onion and is no longer associated with it. Liken the orange to us and the onion to pornography. Explain that allowing corrupt thoughts, ideas, or images to enter our lives, even briefly, can leave lasting effects.

Further explain that complete and true repentance can restore our purity completely so that we can be found worthy to live with Heavenly Father again.

Scripture References

Isaiah 52:11; Doctrine and Covenants 101:97.

Avoiding Temptation

Objective

To demonstrate that the best way to avoid sin is to immediately flee from its presence.

Materials Needed

A bowl of water, ground pepper, and a very small amount of liquid dishwashing soap.

Procedure

Set the bowl of water in the middle of the table or on the floor where everyone can easily see the water.

Generously sprinkle pepper onto the water. Liken the pepper to us, and briefly discuss sin and the necessity of avoiding it as much as possible. Tell class members that we should act like the pepper when we are around temptation or sin. Drop a very small amount of liquid soap into the middle of the water. The pepper will rapidly separate to the sides of the bowl. Stress that quickly fleeing from temptation will help us avoid sin.

Scripture References

Genesis 39:7–12; 1 Timothy 6:11.

Book of Mormon

Objective

To understand one reason why the Book of Mormon is important to us.

Materials Needed

A map of your state or country and a map of a city within your state or country.

Procedure

Explain to the class that you have two maps: one of the state or country and one of a city. Ask: Which map would be needed to find a particular street in the city? Explain that the state or country map is important because it gives a broader view of the area around the city and where it lies in the larger geographic area. However, the city map gives detailed information and would be the map to use.

Compare the city map to the Book of Mormon. This book was written specifically for us and our needs. It gives us vital details on the fulness of the gospel. Point out that, like the state or country map, the Bible gives a more general description of the gospel and a historical account of some of God's children.

Scripture Reference

Doctrine and Covenants 20:7–12.

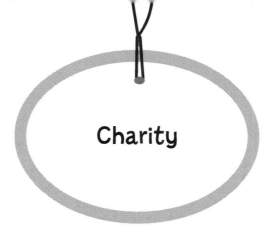

Charity

Objective

To encourage us to seek for the gift of charity in order to bless the lives of others.

Materials Needed

A clear cup and a small pitcher of water.

Procedure

Display the empty cup and explain that the cup is perfectly good and useful. However, to someone who is thirsty, an empty cup without water would be worthless. Fill the cup with water. Explain how the cup filled with simple water could sustain life.

Likewise, when we are filled with charity, we can be good and useful servants for our Heavenly Father to bless the lives of others. When we have charity, we can serve more fully and completely as the Savior would serve.

Scripture Reference

Moroni 7:45–48.

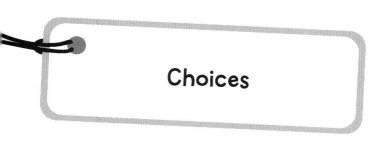

Choices

Objective

To help class members understand that each choice we make helps determine our future.

Materials Needed

Magnetic alphabet letters and a metal board, or a whiteboard and markers.

Procedure

Explain that with a full set of letters we can create many words. After we determine the word we want, we can find the appropriate letters that will spell it. Show a couple of examples on the board. Explain that if we had enough letters we could write a book.

Explain that, in a sense, each of us is writing a book: the book of our future. However, instead of using letters and words, our future is compiled of choices we make. Agency allows us to be the author of our books, because no one else can write our future for us. However, to write a successful ending to our book, we must first decide how we want it to end. Then we must make choices every day that will lead to that ending.

Help class members understand that sometimes we might make a wrong choice which brings conflict and unhappiness, but Jesus Christ provided a way to erase that error and resolve the conflict so we can continue to write and achieve our happy ending.

Scripture Reference

2 Nephi 10:23.

Choices

Objective

To encourage us to choose things which are good for us.

Materials Needed

An apple and a cookie.

Procedure

Invite a group member to help you. Select someone whose strength is the same or less than yours. Ask the volunteer to raise one arm straight out to the side, shoulder level. Place the apple in the outstretched hand and instruct him or her to keep the arm in place as you apply pressure to push the arm down. Use two fingers and apply firm pressure to the arm. The volunteer will be able to keep it in place. Next, replace the apple with the cookie and repeat the procedure exactly. The person's arm will have very little strength or resistance, and you will be able to push it down.

Use this to illustrate that choosing those things which are good for us will strengthen us. However, if we participate in or use things which are not good for us, we become weak and less capable of resisting Satan.

Scripture References

Articles of Faith 1:13; Doctrine and Covenants 89:18–21.

Commandments

Objective
To teach us that obeying the commandments will protect us.

Materials Needed
A cabinet safety latch, safety gate, or childproof lid.

Procedure
Display the safety item you have selected. Discuss its purpose with the group. Point out that it is not intended to unnecessarily restrict a child; rather it is used to protect a child from harmful areas or hazardous materials. The item is designed to provide safety.

Similarly, Heavenly Father gives us commandments in order to keep us safe. His purpose is not to randomly restrict, but instead to protect us from the dangers of temptation and sin. Heavenly Father demonstrates his love for us by giving us commandments.

Scripture References
Proverbs 19:16; Doctrine and Covenants 98:22.

Communication

Objective

To demonstrate the effects of positive interaction with others.

Materials Needed

A piece of silver, a soft cloth, silver polish, and a steel wool pad.

Procedure

Display the piece of silver and cleaning products. Ask: Which cleaning materials should be used to keep the silver shiny and bright? Discuss the results of using the steel wool pad (the silver could become discolored, marred, scratched, etc.). Compare the results of using the silver polish (wipes away smudges, keeps the color bright, preserves shine and value, etc.).

Explain that communication with others is like the silver and must be handled carefully. Gossiping, criticizing, yelling, and belittling are as harsh to a person as the steel wool would be to the silver. These negative forms of communication can destroy another's self-esteem and confidence. This can also hamper their earthly progression.

Positive communication such as honest praise, recognition, soft voices, and uplifting vocabulary can be just as effective as the polish is to the silver. Uplifting communication can build another's self-worth or enhance his or her ability to achieve in life. Our methods of communication may influence others for many years after the original contact. We must carefully choose our words and actions to be a positive influence.

Scripture Reference

Ephesians 4:29–32.

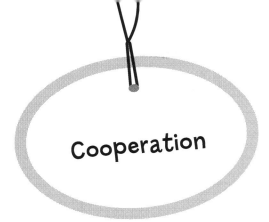

Cooperation

Objective

To show that cooperation leads to solutions.

Materials Needed

A large picture or a scripture printed on a large sheet of paper.

Preparation

Cut the picture or scripture into several pieces, like a puzzle.

Procedure

Give every class member at least one piece of the puzzle and ask them to look at their own piece but not show it to others. Ask: What is the picture or scripture? Why can't you identify it?

Explain that with some challenges or problems, we can only see part of the picture. This can make it difficult to come up with a solution.

Now ask everyone to work on the puzzle together. When the puzzle is completed, discuss how easily it was solved with cooperation.

Scripture Reference

Mosiah 18:21.

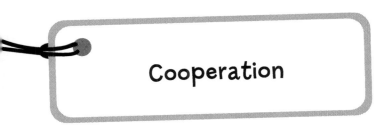

Cooperation

Objective

To show that difficult things can be accomplished when we stand together.

Materials Needed

Twenty to thirty wooden toothpicks and a rubber band.

Procedure

Take one toothpick and try to stand it upright. Express the difficulty of that task. Now take the remaining toothpicks and gather them together in one group. Wrap them with the rubber band to secure them together.

Explain that we are like the toothpicks. When we stand and work together, we can accomplish many things that are difficult.

Scripture Reference

Amos 3:3.

Deception

Objective

To illustrate how easily we can be deceived.

Materials Needed

A paper with an arrow drawn on it and a mirror.

Procedure

Suggest that if we were lost, the most important thing we would need would be directions to point the way home. Hold up the arrow so that it points to either the right or the left. Explain that Heavenly Father gives us directions which we can trust to lead us back home. Satan desires to stop us from returning home. He will do anything he can to deceive us and point us in the wrong direction.

Hold the mirror next to the arrow, angling them slightly so that the arrow is reflected in the mirror. The reflected image will point the opposite way that the arrow points. Explain that although Satan's deceptions may appear real, they actually direct us away from our heavenly home. Instead, the Holy Ghost is a source of truth which will lead us on the correct path to eternal life.

Scripture References

Doctrine and Covenants 45:57; Moses 4:4.

Developing Christlike Attributes

Objective

To illustrate that we become more like Christ as we closely follow his example.

Materials Needed

Several leaves, two sheets of paper for each person, and crayons.

Procedure

Show the group a leaf. Pass out paper and crayons and ask them to draw a picture of the leaf as accurately as possible. When the drawing is finished, give each individual a leaf. Have them cover their leaf with the second piece of paper and color lightly over it to create a leaf rubbing. Discuss which image is a closer replica and why. Using the leaf as a direct pattern produces a very similar likeness.

Compare this to our efforts to become like Christ and develop his attributes. By developing a close relationship with him through study, prayer, and obedience, we can become more like him. Over time, his likeness or image will even show in our countenances.

Scripture References

Doctrine and Covenants 19:23; Alma 5:19.

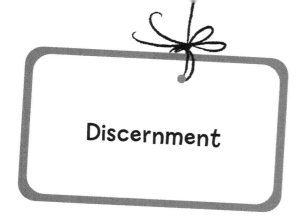

Discernment

Objective

To illustrate the importance of recognizing the true principles of the gospel.

Materials Needed

A dollar bill and a piece of "play" money.

Procedure

Display the genuine money and the play money. Ask: Which currency would you use to buy something at a store? Explain that we must use real money to make a purchase. It is important to distinguish between real and imitation in order to get what we want.

Compare this to gospel truths versus Satan's lies. It is important to recognize the truth and avoid deception. Point out that in order to receive the blessings we ultimately desire, we must recognize and apply the truth in our lives.

Scripture Reference

Moroni 7:15–19.

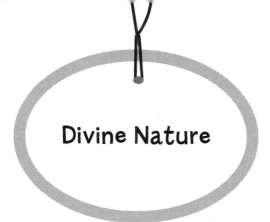

Divine Nature

Objective
To show that all of us have seeds of divine nature within us.

Materials Needed
An apple and a knife.

Procedure
Cut the apple in half widthwise, and show the inner part. Tell the class that every apple has a similar five-sided star inside that holds seeds. Regardless of the condition of the apple (withered, bruised, or ready for picking), the star and its seeds are still inside.

Explain that we are like the apple. Each of us has the potential (seed) of becoming like Heavenly Father. No matter what happens to us, we still have the seeds of divine nature and the potential of godhood.

Scripture References
2 Peter 1:3–4; Acts 17:28.

Divine Potential

Objective

To show that we can become like Heavenly Father.

Materials Needed

A seed package.

Procedure

Show the seeds to the class and explain that these seeds can grow to look like the picture on the front of the package. Read the planting directions on the package and discuss the various things that need to be done to help the seeds grow. Include such things as type of soil, planting time, care, harvest, etc.

Help everyone understand that we are like the seeds. Each of us has the potential of becoming like our heavenly parents because we are their children. Heavenly Father decided when and where we would be placed in our mortal existence. He also chose the conditions which would help us learn the things we need to know to return and live in his presence. Tell the class that Heavenly Father knows our strengths, weaknesses, and abilities, and we were sent to succeed.

Scripture References

Ephesians 5:1; Matthew 5:48.

Endure to the End

Objective

To understand the principle of enduring to the end.

Materials Needed

Enough individually wrapped pieces of taffy and gum for the entire group.

Procedure

Give everyone in the group a piece of taffy. While they are eating the taffy, explain that expectations are often placed upon us, whether for a task, an assignment, or simply a commitment to our standards. We generally start out with a good effort, but after a while, pressures, problems, and obstacles can interfere. Our efforts can begin to dissolve—almost like the taffy that was just eaten.

Hand out gum to the group members. As they chew the gum, explain that we can prove we are made of longer-lasting ingredients if we endure to the end, even through times of pressure and temptation. Compare the principle of endurance to the gum. No matter how many times they apply pressure and chew, the gum still remains. Remind the group that the Lord has promised great things to those who endure to the end.

Scripture References

Doctrine and Covenants 121:8; 2 Timothy 4:7–8.

Enthusiasm

Objective

To inspire us to do what is required with enthusiasm and a good attitude.

Materials Needed

Hot and cold tap water, two bowls, food coloring, and an eye-dropper.

Procedure

Fill one bowl with very hot tap water and the other bowl with very cold tap water. Wait just long enough for the water to stop moving. Then quickly add three drops of food coloring into each bowl. Point out that the food coloring spreads rapidly in the hot water and more slowly in the cold water.

Liken the hot water to enthusiasm and a good attitude. Explain that if we quickly jump into a job with a positive attitude, we can do the task quickly and enjoy the process. If we dread, put off, or complain about our job, we're like the cold water. The job can become a long and agonizing process.

Scripture References

Galatians 4:18; Doctrine and Covenants 58:27.

Example

Objective

To encourage us to set a good example for others.

Materials Needed

A magnifying glass.

Procedure

Discuss with the group how a magnifying glass works. If the group is small enough, let each person use the magnifying glass to view the tiny details of any object.

Explain that as Church members we are often "under a magnifying glass" and our actions are under close inspection by the world. Discuss the importance of setting a good example at all times. We may not know when someone is closely watching us.

Scripture Reference

Matthew 5:14–16.

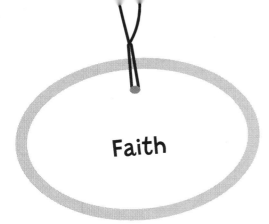

Faith

Objective

To show that faith is believing things that we know but do not necessarily see.

Materials Needed

Ice cubes and a bowl.

Preparation

Place the ice cubes in the bowl just before class begins.

Procedure

Show the class the bowl filled with ice cubes. Ask: What will happen if the bowl is left in a warm room? (The ice will melt.) How do you know?

Tell class members that just as they know the ice will melt, they can also know of God's existence and love for them. Ask class members to share how they feel God's love for them.

Scripture References

Hebrews 11:1; Alma 30:41, 44; 2 Corinthians 5:7.

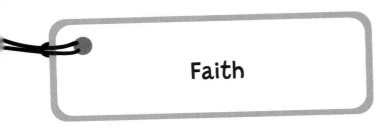

Faith

Objective
To gain an understanding of the true meaning of faith.

Materials Needed
Paper and a small treat or reward.

Preparation
This lesson involves a treasure hunt. Before the lesson, prepare and hide several papers with clues on them. These clues should lead the class members from one place to the next, finally ending with the discovery of a reward.

Procedure
Tell the group that somewhere you have hidden a special reward for them. Hand them the first clue, and tell them that following the clues will lead them to their reward.

After they have completed the treasure hunt and found the reward, sit down and have a short discussion. Ask: How did you know there was a reward at the end of the treasure hunt? (They believed what you told them.) If you believed there was a reward but didn't follow the clues or directions, would you have gotten the reward? (No.) Point out that the class members' beliefs plus their actions helped them receive their reward.

Explain that faith uses this same principle. Heavenly Father has told us that there is a wonderful reward waiting for us. If we believe him but don't follow the instructions he has provided, we'll never find that reward. If we believe him and then take action, strictly following the directions, we will receive the reward. Belief plus action equals faith.

Scripture References

3 Nephi 13:20–21; Alma 32:43.

Faith

Objective

To demonstrate the importance of faith.

Materials Needed

A quart jar of water and a Ping-Pong ball.

Procedure

Display the jar of water and drop the Ping-Pong ball into it. Using your finger, try to push the ball under water several times. Point out that the ball always pops back up to the surface. Ask: What would happen if I poked a hole in the ball? (Over time, water would seep in, and the ball would sink to the bottom.)

Compare this demonstration to having faith. If we exercise faith in Jesus Christ, our trials will have no power to bring us down. It is only if we let fear or doubt seep in that trials have power to overcome us.

Scripture Reference

Matthew 14:25–33.

Following Christ

Objective

To encourage us to follow the Savior.

Materials Needed

A vase of sunflowers or a picture of a sunflower.

Procedure

Show the sunflowers. Tell the group that the sunflower waits patiently through the night until the sun appears in the morning. Then the sunflower follows the course of the sun throughout the day, and at nightfall it returns to its original position and once again waits for the sunrise.

Explain that we should be like the sunflower in our loyalty to and undeviating faith in Jesus Christ, the Son of God. Discuss ways that we can stay focused on the Savior and remember him throughout the day. Consider the following ideas: prayer, scripture study, obedience, gospel covenants, and so forth.

Scripture References

Matthew 4:19–20; Moroni 4:3; 5:2.

Following Christ

Objective
To illustrate the importance of a Christ-centered life.

Materials Needed
A picture of the solar system.

Procedure
Display the picture of the solar system and show that the sun is the center of our solar system with all the planets revolving around it. Discuss how the rotation and revolution of the Earth ensure constant light and heat on our planet.

Explain that the Savior offers us the spiritual light (truth) and warmth (love) that we need to guide us. Point out that to enjoy the full benefit of the Savior's light and warmth we must keep him at the center of our lives. We demonstrate his importance by revolving our lives around him. Discuss how this can be done. Ideas might include prayer, scripture study, temple attendance, and obedience.

Scripture Reference
John 8:12.

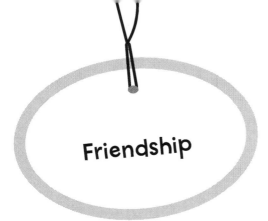

Friendship

Objective

To show that our associations with other people can "rub off."

Materials Needed

Chalk dust.

Procedure

After "chalking" your hands, show them to the class. Ask: What would happen if I shook hands with you or patted you on the back? Discuss.

Explain that friendship is much like the chalk dust. As we associate with friends, their good or bad qualities can rub off on us. Discuss how having a good friend can really support a person. Discuss what makes a good friend.

Additional Idea

Discuss how to be a good friend and why it is important.

Scripture Reference

Proverbs 22:24–25.

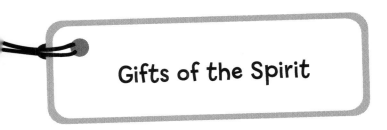

Gifts of the Spirit

Objective

To show that our gifts and talents, although different, are equally important in blessing the lives of those around us.

Materials Needed

Several different kinds of fruit.

Procedure

Show the fruit to class members. Talk about what makes each fruit different from the others. Tell the class you are not looking for differences in outward appearances. After a brief discussion, help the class understand that each fruit provides different vitamins and minerals and all have equal importance for different reasons.

Liken the fruit to each of us. All of us have different talents or gifts of the Spirit, but all are equally important in blessing the lives of others.

Scripture References

Doctrine and Covenants 46:11; 1 Corinthians 12:4.

Gifts of the Spirit

Objective

To encourage us to use our gifts of the Spirit.

Materials Needed

A cake mix and a prepared cake.

Procedure

Display the cake mix and the prepared cake. Compare the cake mix to the gifts of the Spirit. Explain that the cake cannot be enjoyed by others until it is mixed, baked, and served. Similarly, we must put forth effort to develop and use our individual gifts in order to bless the lives of others. Just as there are specific steps to bake a cake, there are also specific things we must do to expand our gifts and talents. These things might include prayer, practice, and seeking opportunities to use the gifts.

Serve the prepared cake and discuss the importance of dedicating our efforts to magnify our gifts and share them with others. Emphasize that the gifts of the Spirit are given for the purpose of blessing Heavenly Father's children.

Scripture Reference

Doctrine and Covenants 46:8–12.

Goals

Objective
To illustrate the process of setting and achieving goals.

Materials Needed
A jigsaw puzzle with hundreds of pieces.

Procedure
Ask if it would be possible for a member of the group to complete the puzzle in five minutes. Of course not; a complicated puzzle requires sorting, studying, and carefully piecing it together. It may take a long time, but the process can be enjoyable and the finished product will be a beautiful, interesting image.

Discuss the similarities between completing the puzzle and setting and achieving goals. Consider the steps of selecting a goal, determining specific steps, working diligently, recording progress, and following through until completion. These steps take time. However, the process can be as enjoyable as the successful achievement of the goal.

Scripture Reference
Doctrine and Covenants 58:27.

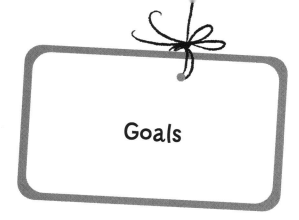

Goals

Objective

To show that an assignment is more effectively accomplished when organized into several smaller goals than in one large event.

Materials Needed

Seven coins.

Procedure

Tell the class that you have seven coins. Ask one person to catch the coins when you throw them. Tell him to catch as many as he can. Toss the coins all at once to the catcher. Ask: How many coins did you catch? Gather the coins and then toss them one at a time. Ask: How many coins did you catch this time?

Explain that the coins are like goals, assignments, or tasks to be completed. When we try to take on too many things at one time, some may not be accomplished (or caught). By careful planning, more goals will be effectively completed when taken one at a time.

Scripture References

1 Corinthians 14:40; Mosiah 4:27.

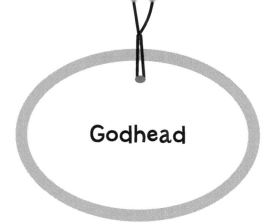

Godhead

Objective

To illustrate that Heavenly Father, Jesus Christ, and the Holy Ghost work together to fulfill one purpose.

Materials Needed

A large triangle made from construction paper or poster board.

Procedure

Post the triangle so it is visible to the entire group. Explain that the triangle is one of the strongest shapes known to man. It is often used in architecture. Buildings, bridges, and other structures use the design of the triangle for reinforcement and strength. The triangle is strong because each side reinforces the other.

Point out the similarities between the triangle and the Godhead. The Godhead consists of three separate members—Heavenly Father, Jesus Christ, and the Holy Ghost—who work together for one purpose. Label each side of the triangle with a corresponding member of the Godhead. Then write "Moses 1:39" in the center of the triangle. Read the scripture together and discuss what each member of the Godhead does or has done to "bring to pass the immortality and eternal life of man."

Scripture Reference

Moses 1:39.

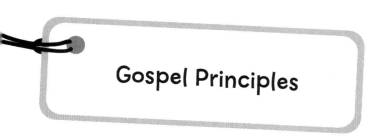

Gospel Principles

Objective
To encourage us to always live the principles of the gospel.

Materials Needed
A coat.

Procedure
Explain that coats are designed to keep us warm and to protect us from the cold. Yet they can only offer this service if we wear them. Sometimes we don't want to take the time to put one on; other times we don't want to be encumbered with a coat; still other times we are embarrassed to wear one because it isn't fashionable. So we deny ourselves the comfort our coats could give us, and instead we suffer with the cold.

Point out that living the principles of the gospel is similar to wearing a coat. The gospel can protect and comfort us throughout our earth life. Yet at times we may not make the effort to live these principles. Sometimes we may feel that the principles are too restrictive or burdensome. Or we may feel that living by these standards is not fashionable. It is important to recognize and use the protection and comfort that we can receive as we faithfully live the principles of the gospel.

Scripture Reference
Articles of Faith 1:4.

Gospel Teaching

Objective

To show how teaching the gospel to others helps them reach their full potential.

Materials Needed

A package of dehydrated food.

Procedure

Show the dehydrated food to the group. Ask: What does this dehydrated food need? (Water.) When water is added, the food expands and reaches its full potential.

Explain that as we teach others the principles of the gospel, we offer them the water which will expand their understanding, enlarge their testimonies, and increase their ability to live righteous lives. Teaching the gospel helps other people reach their full potential as sons and daughters of God.

Scripture Reference

Doctrine and Covenants 10:66.

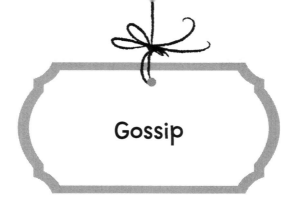

Gossip

Objective

To demonstrate the difficulty of gathering the effects of gossip.

Materials Needed

Down feathers (any easily blown object will do), wind or a fan, and a paper sack.

Preparation

Although this lesson works best outside, it can be used indoors with a fan.

Procedure

Have the class sit in an open area outside. Place the feathers into the paper sack and give the sack to one student. Allow the student to open the bag and let the feathers drop in an open area, but insist that the feathers must not go any further.

Briefly discuss how gossip is like the feathers. It is easily taken out into the open, and once let out, it is free to spread anywhere, even if people are specifically instructed to keep it to themselves and not let it go any further. Tell the students to collect all the feathers. After they return, ask: How easy was it to gather the feathers?

Explain that, like the feathers, gossip is easily shared or released but very difficult to gather back.

Scripture Reference

2 Timothy 2:16.

Habits

Objective

To show that habits are harder to break the more they are used.

Materials Needed

Sewing thread and two sticks.

Procedure

Have one individual hold the two sticks about six to twelve inches apart. Wind the thread around the two sticks once and tie. Ask the class member to break the thread. Next, wind the thread around the stick three times and ask him or her to break the string. Add layers of string as you repeat the process until the string cannot be broken. Ask: What is the difference between the first and last time?

Explain that habits, both good and bad, are like the string. Habits can be easily broken when new, but they are difficult to stop after repeated use.

This demonstration can focus on either good or bad habits. Explain that bad habits should be broken early and good habits should be encouraged and strengthened through use.

Scripture Reference

Titus 2:7.

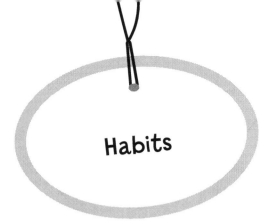

Habits

Objective
To illustrate that daily actions lead to habits.

Materials Needed
Dominoes.

Procedure
Stand the dominoes on end in a line, one behind the other. Explain that when the first domino is knocked down, it will in turn knock down another, and then another, and so on.

Explain that habits work in the same way. One action leads to another. This develops into a pattern which, once started, is hard to stop. Both good and bad habits are formed this way. Push over the first domino to set the falling line of dominoes into action to illustrate the point.

Scripture Reference
Luke 9:23.

Helping Others

Objective

To help class members understand that our own imperfections can affect how well we can help others.

Materials Needed

Toothpaste, two pairs of non-prescription eyeglasses or sunglasses, one large paper with a fairly simple line pattern, pencils, and paper.

Preparation

Liberally smear toothpaste on the lenses of one pair of glasses.

Procedure

Choose four class members and split them into two sets of partners. Tell them that one partner will draw and the other will explain what a pattern looks like. Give a pencil and paper to the two people who will draw, and have them sit with their backs to the class. Give each explainer a pair of glasses to wear. Once their glasses are on, place the patterned paper where it cannot be seen by those who will draw. Have the explainers tell their partners what to draw. Show the finished product to the class.

As the class looks at the drawings, liken the process to helping others. Explain that if our spiritual vision is impaired we cannot always help others as effectively. Ask: What things would affect our ability to help other people? (Prejudice, personal sin, intolerance, miscommunication, etc.) List their ideas on the board and discuss.

Scripture Reference

Matthew 7:3–5.

Holy Ghost

Objective

To help class members understand that the Holy Ghost comforts and surrounds us with peace.

Materials Needed

A large, soft quilt or comforter.

Procedure

Wrap yourself in the quilt and refer to it as a comforter. Explain that people call it a comforter because it is soft and warm and can help us feel very comfortable.

Teach that the Comforter is also another name for the Holy Ghost. Ask: Why would the Holy Ghost be called a comforter? Explain that the Holy Ghost can help us feel comfortable when we allow his influence to surround our lives.

Scripture References

Doctrine and Covenants 36:2; John 14:26–27.

Holy Ghost

Objective

To illustrate how we learn to recognize the promptings of the Holy Ghost.

Materials Needed

A poster board and marking pen.

Preparation

Write a word or sentence in a foreign language on the poster board.

Procedure

Display the sentence and ask if anyone can read it. If no one is able to interpret the sentence, translate it for them. Point out that understanding a foreign language requires time and effort. Discuss what must be done to master another language. Consider the following ideas: desire, commitment, good teachers, textbooks, and use of the new language.

Explain that learning to understand the promptings of the Spirit is similar to learning another language. Recognizing the guidance of the Spirit requires time and effort. Discuss ideas that would assist in this process. These might include prayer, fasting, scripture study, pondering, and obeying. As we endeavor to seek and follow the promptings of the Holy Ghost, we will learn to recognize more clearly the still, small voice.

Scripture References

John 14:26; Doctrine and Covenants 9:7–9.

Humility

Objective

To demonstrate the importance of humility as we seek to follow the Savior.

Materials Needed

A lump of soft clay and a lump of hardened clay.

Procedure

Show the group how the soft clay can be molded into any shape you desire. Then try to mold the hardened clay. Show that the hardened clay is unworkable and impossible to shape.

Similarly, we are like the clay. When we are humble and teachable, Heavenly Father can shape and mold us to become more Christlike. If we are prideful, we harden ourselves to the guiding influences of the Lord and become unworkable. Discuss ways that we can become more humble and teachable.

Scripture References

Ether 12:27; Isaiah 64:8.

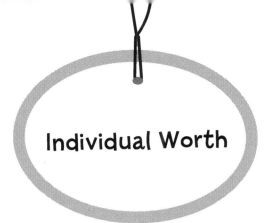

Individual Worth

Objective
To encourage us to value others.

Materials Needed
A jigsaw puzzle.

Procedure
Display the jigsaw puzzle. Point out that although each of the pieces are different, they all fit together to form a beautiful picture. Ask the group to consider the disappointment and frustration that would occur after putting the puzzle together and discovering one piece to be missing.

Explain that as children of our Heavenly Father, each of us is different. However, as we all work together we can accomplish many wonderful things. Each of us is an important part of a divine picture. The absence of even one individual leaves this picture incomplete.

Variation
Distribute all the pieces of a small jigsaw puzzle and then assemble it together to illustrate how each member of the group must contribute to make the picture complete.

Scripture Reference
Doctrine and Covenants 18:10.

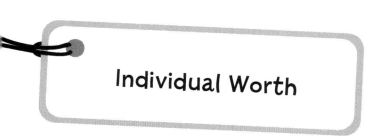

Individual Worth

Objective
To help us accept the differences in others.

Materials Needed
Three different types of fruit.

Procedure
Display the fruit and ask: Which fruit is the best? Discuss the merits of each, such as calories, nutrients, appearance, flavor, and so on. Also consider personal favorites. Explain that even though you might like one kind of fruit better than another, it does not take away from the value of the other fruits.

Likewise, people may differ in personality, physical appearance, talents, or needs. However, these differences do not lessen their individual value as a child of God.

Scripture References
Doctrine and Covenants 18:10; Acts 10:34–35.

Integrity

Objective

To show why regular maintenance of our integrity is important.

Materials Needed

Building blocks.

Preparation

Label each block with a positive characteristic of integrity.

Procedure

As you build a wall of building blocks, explain that personal integrity is made of small, everyday actions that help build a barricade against Satan. As we actively increase and maintain our integrity, the barricade becomes thicker and higher. Continue to build the wall.

Then point out that Satan's ultimate plan is to completely destroy our barricade of integrity so that he can control us. To achieve this he first weakens the outside, the seemingly nonessential part of our integrity (remove a few outer blocks). As we accept this erosion of our integrity, he begins to take bigger and more important chunks from our integrity (remove or knock down significant portions of the wall of blocks) until the barricade we have carefully built crumbles.

Our goal, then, is to continually strengthen our wall of integrity and to never give Satan a chance to weaken it. Discuss ways to build and maintain personal integrity.

Scripture Reference

Alma 53:20.

Inviting the Spirit

Objective

To show that through obedient and thoughtful actions, we invite the Spirit into our lives.

Materials Needed

Several battery powered tea lights.

Procedure

If possible, darken the room slightly. Turn on one tea light and place it in the middle of the table. Ask: What things can you do daily to invite the Spirit? (Pray, read scriptures, serve others, etc.) As each idea is shared, turn on another tea light and place it by the first one. When all the lights have been used, ask what would happen if more tea lights were turned on.

Liken the tea lights to the Spirit of the Lord. As we obey the commandments and participate in spiritual activities, we invite the Spirit and bring light into our lives.

Scripture References

Moroni 7:16; Doctrine and Covenants 50:24.

Jesus Christ, Savior

Objective

To help class members understand that Jesus Christ is the only means by which we can return to Heavenly Father.

Materials Needed

Two small pieces of PVC pipe (same size) and a coupler that will link them together.

Procedure

Ask: What should be our ultimate goal in life? (To return to live with Heavenly Father.) Show the two pieces of PVC pipe to the group. Liken one to us and the other to Heavenly Father. Point out that there is no way that these two pieces can join together by themselves.

Show the PVC coupler and liken it to Jesus Christ, who is our mediator. Show how the coupler is used to bring the two pieces together. Explain that Christ made it possible for us to return to Heavenly Father through his Atonement. Only through his sacrifice can we receive eternal life. As we believe in him, keep his commandments, and repent, we can return to Heavenly Father.

Scripture References

John 14:6; Mosiah 3:17.

Judgment

Objective

To show that outward appearances are not always as they seem.

Materials Needed

Sugar cookies, regular icing, and salted icing.

Preparation

Prepare a small batch of icing, using seven to eight times more salt than called for in the recipe. Ice several cookies with this salty icing, and decorate them. (These cookies could also be made with salted dough.) Ice and decorate the rest of the cookies with regular icing. Make enough regular cookies for the entire class plus additional salted cookies. Arrange an equal number of salted and regular cookies mixed together on the same plate, with just enough for the entire class. Set aside extra regular cookies to replace the salted ones.

Procedure

Show the plate of cookies to the class. Pass the cookies around as you would a treat. Quietly watch for reactions. Those with salted cookies will show surprise or may openly complain. Explain that people are like the cookies. Outward appearances are not always accurate in judging people or their actions. If we judge based on outward appearances, we may be in for a surprise. Give a regular sugar cookie to those who originally received salted cookies so all can enjoy the treat.

Note

A beautifully decorated Styrofoam cake could be used instead of cookies.

Scripture Reference

3 Nephi 14:15, 20.

Knowledge

Objective

To help us learn the importance of acquiring and using knowledge, both temporal and spiritual.

Materials Needed

Several books relating to a specific topic, such as computer technology, medicine, gardening, or another topic of your choice, and a set of scriptures.

Procedure

Show the topic-specific books to the group. Explain that you would need to carefully study the material in the books to learn about this subject. Discuss other means of acquiring knowledge such as teachers, mentors, and classes. Studying and learning about a subject gives you knowledge. Point out that we don't fully benefit from knowledge until we use it. As we use acquired knowledge in our careers, communities, families, and personal lives, we will experience satisfaction, success, and prosperity.

Display the scriptures. Point out that acquiring spiritual knowledge is similar. We can gain this knowledge through studying the scriptures, listening to the prophet, attending church, and so on. However, we must apply that knowledge in order to receive a fulness of blessings. Discuss ways to apply spiritual knowledge. Consider the following ideas: baptism, priesthood blessings, temple ordinances, obedience, and repentance.

Scripture Reference

2 Timothy 3:15–17.

Leadership

Objective

To show that basic principles of leadership and delegation are necessary to complete a task successfully.

Materials Needed

A recording of a beautifully orchestrated piece of music.

Procedure

Play the music for several minutes. Ask: How many people were necessary to create that piece of music? Include the orchestra members, composer, conductor, sound engineers, etc. Ask: What would happen if there were no composer or sound engineer or orchestra? What would it be like if the conductor tried to do everything? What would happen if orchestra members didn't bother to practice or the sound engineer arrived an hour late? Indicate that each individual plays an important part in the sound of the finished product—even the ones who work behind the scenes.

Liken the music to a ward or branch. There are many people who tirelessly do home teaching and visiting teaching. Others teach in different organizations or organize activities. Still others help through compassionate service or humanitarian efforts. Like the orchestra director, the bishop cannot do all the things that need to be done in the ward, so he delegates many tasks. Briefly discuss the importance of each person helping in the ward.

Scripture Reference

Exodus 18:13–26.

Leadership

Objective

To show that the kind of leadership we give is very important.

Materials Needed

Twelve flat toothpicks, string, and a rubber band.

Procedure

Take the toothpicks and gather them together in a bunch. Do not tie them. Discuss what could be done to help the toothpicks stand up.

Explain that the tooth picks are like a group that needs leadership. This leadership could be offered in three ways:

The careless leader. Tie four toothpicks together very loosely, and try to stand them up. Explain that this leader does not follow up and give encouragement. Consequently, this leader's group will fall down on projects or assignments.

The strict leader. Tie four toothpicks together very tightly. Tie them tightly enough that the toothpicks crack or break. Explain that this leader uses pressure, criticism, or sarcasm to ensure success as a leader.

The flexible leader. Wrap four toothpicks with a rubber band. Explain that this type of leader encourages and follows through on assignments but never binds tightly. This leader is good at give-and-take and considers the needs of the group.

Scripture Reference

Jacob 1:19.

Listening for the Spirit

Objective

To show the importance of having time and peace to listen to the whispering of the Spirit.

Materials Needed

Several electronic devices (such as MP3 player, CD player, radio, cell phone, e-book reader, handheld game, etc.) and scriptures.

Procedure

Turn on the electronic devices, one at a time. Quietly direct the class to turn to 1 Kings 19:9–12 and read it to themselves. Some class members may not hear the instructions. Give the class a few minutes of reading time. Ask: Did the electronic devices make a difference in your scripture reading?

Liken the electronic devices to the business and complexity of the world around us. Explain that sometimes the everyday noises of the world make it difficult to hear the promptings of the Spirit in our lives. Ask: How can we resolve that problem?

Scripture References

1 Kings 19:9–12; Helaman 5:23–50.

Missionary Work

Objective

To show that the gospel is more enjoyable when shared.

Materials Needed

An orange.

Procedure

Tell everyone how good it will be to eat the orange. While peeling the orange, comment on how good it smells and how juicy it is. After the orange is peeled, take some time to admire it. Remove one segment and begin eating it. Express how good it tastes: not too sour, very juicy, and so on. Ask one person: How delicious is the orange? (He or she won't know.) Why don't you know? (Because he or she didn't taste the orange.)

Explain that the gospel is like the orange. Everyone can see that you are enjoying it, but until you share it, others will not know for themselves. Share the orange with the class.

Scripture Reference

Doctrine and Covenants 18:15–16.

Missionary Work

Objective

To illustrate that others can receive the light of the gospel through our missionary efforts.

Materials Needed

A flashlight and a mirror.

Procedure

If possible, slightly darken the room. Turn on the flashlight and place it upright in a central location. Briefly explain to the group that by using the mirror you can reflect the beam of light to each individual in the room. Give a quick demonstration or have a class member help direct the beam with a mirror to touch each member of the class. Explain that it may take time, thought, and effort to get around obstacles and figure which angle to use, but everyone can be reached with the light.

Liken this to missionary work. With Christ as our light source, we act as the mirror which reflects the love and truth he offers. We can reflect this to our Heavenly Father's children. There may be some who appear unapproachable and impossible to reach. Yet they too can receive the gospel light. It may take time and effort as we search for ways to reach them, but with diligence and faith we can be successful.

Scripture Reference

Doctrine and Covenants 45:28.

Moderation

Objective

To show that more is not always better.

Materials Needed

Two pairs of socks.

Procedure

Ask for a volunteer who is wearing socks and thinks they have very comfortable shoes. Ask that person to take off his or her shoes. Ask: Do your socks make your shoes more comfortable? Give the volunteer another pair of socks to put on over their own socks. Suggest that if one pair of socks makes shoes more comfortable, a second pair should be even better. When that pair has been put on, instruct the volunteer to add a third pair. Have them put their comfortable shoes back on and ask: How do your shoes feel?

Liken the socks to things we might find in life that make us feel comfortable. We must realize that having more doesn't always make us happy. In addition, if we love something so much that we constantly think and talk about it, we may appear excessive. When we avoid excessive behavior we are referred to as "moderate." Moderate people have learned to control their actions. Ask: How can you show moderation?

Scripture Reference

Alma 38:10.

Obedience

Objective

To illustrate that we draw closer to the Lord through obedience to the covenants we make with him.

Materials Needed

A large picture of Christ glued to poster board, three sheets of different colored cellophane or vellum, one clear sheet of cellophane, and two individual binder rings. (Most florists or craft stores have cellophane.)

Preparation

Trim the cellophane to be the same size as the poster board. Punch two holes in the top of the poster board and in corresponding places on each piece of cellophane. Layer the cellophane on top of the poster, with the clear piece directly against the picture. Fasten the cellophane and poster together with the rings. Place the visual aid on an easel.

Procedure

Introduce the topic of obedience to covenants we make with the Lord. Discuss different types of covenants and what we can do to keep them: baptism, endowment, and sealing. Explain that if we are faithful to our baptismal covenants, we will draw closer to the Savior, and the veil that separates us will be thinned. Pull back the first sheet of cellophane. The picture of Christ will look a little clearer. Repeat the process for the other two covenants. All that will cover the picture at this point is the clear cellophane. Use this visual aid to illustrate how thin the veil can become and how close we can draw to the Savior through obedience.

Scripture Reference

Doctrine and Covenants 88:63.

Obedience

Objective

To illustrate that obedience to God's commandments provides boundaries to protect us and to help us become better people.

Materials Needed

Two loaves of frozen bread dough, one bread pan, and one large piece of aluminum foil.

Preparation

Allow the two loaves of bread dough to rise, one loaf in a regular bread pan and the other loaf on a counter. Before baking, transfer the second loaf to a piece of aluminum foil. The dough will probably become slightly misshapen as it is moved. Bake the two loaves of bread.

Procedure

Display the two loaves of bread and ask the class to enumerate the differences. Acknowledge that one was baked in a bread pan and the other on a piece of aluminum foil.

Liken us to the bread dough and the bread pan to God's commandments. Explain that the commandments provide boundaries and keep us safe. We become better people when we are obedient to those commandments because we allow righteousness to shape our heart and soul.

Scripture Reference

Doctrine and Covenants 98:22.

Ordinances of the Gospel

Objective

To gain a greater understanding of the saving ordinances of the gospel.

Materials Needed

A set of four keys.

Procedure

Display the keys. Explain that the keys represent the saving ordinances of the gospel. Receiving the keys represents our participation in the sacred acts of the ordinances. Actually using the keys to unlock each consecutive door illustrates that we are living righteously, continually worthy of the promised blessings. Point out that obtaining and using these keys must be done in order.

Take the first key and explain that it represents baptism. When we are baptized, we receive a key which can be used to unlock a door on our journey back to Heavenly Father.

The second key is the priesthood. Although it is received and held by men, it must be shared with women and family members to unlock the second door on our journey.

The third key is temple endowments. This key unlocks another door, enabling us to draw closer to our Father in Heaven.

The last key is temple marriage. With this key we unlock the final door on our journey to return home.

Scripture Reference

Articles of Faith 1:3.

Patriarchal Blessing

Objective

To illustrate that our patriarchal blessings are loving instructions from our Father in Heaven.

Materials Needed

An addressed, stamped envelope with a letter inside.

Procedure

Have the class members imagine themselves far away in a foreign land. They have been away for a long time and feel lonely and isolated. Show the envelope with an enclosed letter. Have them imagine their joy at receiving a letter from home. They'd most likely read it again and again, savoring every word.

Explain that, in a sense, we are strangers in a foreign land, but we have the opportunity to receive a very special letter from home—one which offers divine guidance, instructions, and encouragement. This letter is a patriarchal blessing, and it is sent from our Heavenly Father to a child whom he loves dearly.

Scripture Reference

Isaiah 63:7.

Peace

Objective

To encourage harmony at home.

Materials Needed

A pot, a large serving spoon, a delicate goblet or glass, and a small teaspoon.

Procedure

Begin by taking the large spoon and banging the pot loudly several times. Then take the teaspoon and carefully tap the glass, producing a delicate ringing sound.

Point out that nagging, criticizing, shouting, and name-calling are much the same as banging the pot. They hurt our ears and make us want to avoid the sounds as much as possible.

In contrast, the tinkling sound of the glass can be compared to cheerfulness, encouragement, and displays of love. Those pleasant sounds are appealing and encourage the listener to yearn for more. Explain that through controlling our voice and attitude we can make our home a haven where family members desire to be.

Scripture Reference

Proverbs 16:24.

Personal Evaluation

Objective

To show the importance of personal evaluation in the refining process.

Materials Needed

A small container of sand mixed with debris (twigs and grasses), strainer, and a tray.

Procedure

Show the container of sand. Explain that clean sand, when combined with cement mix and water, can make a strong concrete that will set up hard without cracks or faults. Tell the class that when there is debris in the sand, it weakens the concrete and can eventually result in weaknesses and cracks.

Study and evaluate the sand with the class. Determine together that the sand has some debris in it and needs some refining before it can be used. Explain that it needs to be run through the strainer to be refined. Help them understand that cleaning the sand can be time consuming, but it is worth the effort to make the finished product exceptional. Put the tray on the table and hold the strainer above it. Pour some sand through the strainer into the tray. Show the class the debris that remains after sifting the first batch.

Liken this process to our lives. We are like the sand with some debris in it. We are given mortality, this time on earth, to refine ourselves. Tell them that before we can refine ourselves, we must personally evaluate and determine what must be done. Ask: What questions could we ask ourselves to evaluate the type of refining we need? Help them understand that evaluation is an essential part of the refining process that will take us back to Heavenly Father's presence.

Scripture References

Alma 30:8; Mosiah 4:30.

Priesthood Power

Objective

To understand that the priesthood must have the correct keys to function.

Materials Needed

Car keys.

Procedure

Tell the class to imagine that in the parking lot there is a new car that they can use. Describe the details of the car (horsepower, rate of acceleration, body design, engine size, etc.). State that no matter how powerful the car is, it still depends upon the proper keys to operate.

Explain that priesthood power must also come through the proper authority (keys) in order to function.

Follow up with a discussion of priesthood authority and its functions.

Scripture Reference

Doctrine and Covenants 65:2.

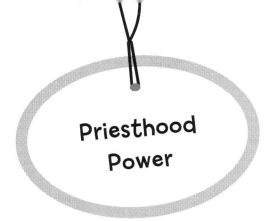

Priesthood Power

Objective

To show that spiritual strength affects ability to use priesthood power.

Materials Needed

Two flashlights—one with good batteries and one with weak or dead batteries.

Procedure

Display the two flashlights, and turn both of them on. Ask: Why doesn't one flashlight work? List possible reasons. Explain that at one time both batteries worked well, but over time one set weakened. Ask: Which flashlight would be most useful in an emergency?

Liken the flashlight to the priesthood and the batteries to spirituality. Explain that spirituality gives strength to the priesthood. Discuss things which can weaken our spiritual strength (such as profanity, pornography, violence, rebelliousness, inappropriate music or movies, etc.). Express how important it would be to have a worthy priesthood holder during a time of need.

Additional Idea

Discuss ways that spirituality can be increased.

Scripture Reference

Doctrine and Covenants 121:41–45.

Priorities

Objective

To show that we can lose the most important parts of the gospel in everyday living.

Materials Needed

A statue or picture of Jesus Christ and several light scarves or pieces of sheer fabric.

Procedure

Place the statue of Christ in the center of an uncluttered table. Tell the class how important Christ is in your life and how much you want to always listen to and follow him. Then tell them that you would like to tell them about a typical day in your life.

Tell a story about a very busy and hectic day. Fill it with good activities (Relief Society meeting, taking children to music lessons, fixing a bike for a child, making a birthday cake, attending an adult education class, exercising, priesthood activity, etc.). Be sure not to include time for prayer, scripture study, or compassionate service. As you tell about each activity, drape a scarf or piece of fabric over the statue of Christ. Do this until you have finished with the entire day.

Explain to the class that you had a day filled with good "gospel-approved" activities, but the real center of the gospel was covered with the busy things of life. Prayer, scripture study, meditation, compassionate service, all the things that help us listen to the promptings of the Spirit and draw us closer to Jesus Christ—the truly important things—were not included.

Discuss how setting priorities can ensure that the most important gospel activities are not covered up by all the other busy details of daily living.

Scripture Reference
Matthew 6:33.

Priorities

Objective

To show that thoughtfully prioritizing tasks and organizing our time enables us to accomplish more.

Materials Needed

A large glass container, a pitcher of water, and several oranges (or other type of fruit).

Preparation

This object lesson is most effective when you have practiced and know the maximum number of oranges and the amount of water needed to fit within the glass container.

Procedure

Using the water in the pitcher, fill the glass container half to three-quarters full of water and display it for the class. Explain that the container represents our lives and the water represents all the everyday activities that can keep us busy. Invite class members to list different things that might fall into this category (school, homework, friends, video games, Internet, family history, television, work, etc). Help class members understand that some of the items mentioned are good things to do, while others are more for enjoyment. Indicate that, because the container is not full, there is still time left for those things that we should do to strengthen us spiritually (indicate the empty part).

Hold up the oranges and ask class members to list things we do to regularly strengthen our spirituality (read scriptures, attend the temple, attend Sunday meetings, participate in family home evening, etc.). Set aside an orange for each idea. After all the fruit has been associated with a suggestion, begin to drop the fruit, one at a time, into the container of water. As the container approaches overflowing, point out the remaining fruit. Discuss the possible side effects of not completing our spiritual strengthening.

Now pour the water back into the pitcher and place all of the fruit into the glass container. Pour water over the fruit until the container is full. Explain that there is still a little water left over but that you have placed all of the fruit in the container.

Tell the class that, in order to get the most out of life, we need to prioritize what is most important and what is least important and schedule our time accordingly. Be sure to include the idea that Heavenly Father wants us to learn, grow, and enjoy our time in mortality. Briefly discuss how to determine which tasks might be most important.

Scripture Reference
Doctrine and Covenants 88:119.

Priorities

Objective

To show the value of concentrating our efforts on the basic priorities in our lives.

Materials Needed

A large red apple and a small red apple.

Procedure

Explain that when an apple tree is loaded with apples in the early summer, the experienced farmer or gardener thins the fruit on the tree and discards a portion of the apples. This keeps the tree limbs from splitting under the heavy burden and enables the tree to provide nutrition to the remaining apples, allowing them to develop into large, juicy apples.

Display the small apple. Explain that sometimes we get busy with too many things and spread ourselves too thin. Then the results are like that of the split limbs and the small apples.

Sometimes it becomes necessary to thin out the activities and time commitments in our lives. By setting priorities and concentrating our efforts on those things, we can have results like the large apple. Display the large apple. Express your hope that the class members' lives will produce good fruit as they focus on those things which matter most.

Scripture References

Doctrine and Covenants 88:119; Mosiah 4:27.

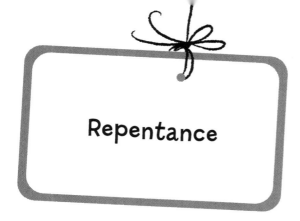

Repentance

Objective

To illustrate why repentance is important.

Materials Needed

A doormat.

Procedure

Display the doormat. Point out that it is put in front of the door to let those who enter wipe the dirt and debris from their feet so they will not soil the inside of the home.

Liken the doormat to repentance. Repentance enables us to remove the things from our lives that are not clean. Explain further that unless we cleanse our lives of such debris, we will not be allowed into our Father's house.

Scripture Reference

3 Nephi 27:19.

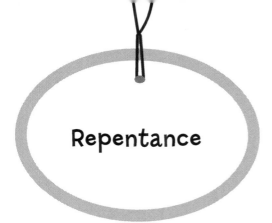

Repentance

Objective

To help class members understand that repentance is necessary to heal the soul.

Materials Needed

First-aid kit.

Procedure

Show the first-aid kit and ask the class what it could be used for. Explain that when someone is hurt it can be an important tool for helping them get better. Ask: What would happen if a serious cut went untreated? (It might get infected, bleed too much, cause more serious problems, etc.). Tell the class that usually we can use a first-aid kit to care for our own little injuries, but when an injury is serious, we must go to someone with more authority and knowledge of first aid and medicine.

Tell the class that sin is like an injury to the spirit. If left untreated, it can also lead to more serious complications. Briefly discuss what some of those complications might be. (More serious sin, apostasy, or spiritual death.) Tell class members that we can take care of most of our spiritual injuries on our own. Discuss how this can be done. Remind them that when the sin is grievous, someone with authority must help us. Ask: Who would that person be? (The bishop.)

Scripture References

Psalm 30:2; Isaiah 53:4–6.

Restored Gospel

Objective

To illustrate the need for the restoration of the gospel.

Materials Needed

Two glasses of water and a small amount of dirt, pebbles, and other debris.

Procedure

Display one glass of clean water. Compare this to the Church which Jesus Christ organized during his mortal ministry. Explain that following his Crucifixion and Resurrection, the gospel continued to be taught. However, after Jesus' apostles were gone and over a period of time, people began adding to and taking away from his gospel. Pour the dirt, pebbles, and other debris into the water. Point out that this polluted the Lord's teachings. It was displeasing to him because these teachings were no longer his pure gospel. The true gospel was no longer on the earth. Take the glass of dirty water away.

After a period of time, through the Prophet Joseph Smith, the Lord restored the gospel in its fulness and purity. Display the second glass of clean water. This is the same gospel that we enjoy today.

Scripture References

2 Nephi 25:17; 2 Thessalonians 2:1–3.

Resurrection

Objective

To visually demonstrate the concepts of premortality, mortality, death, and resurrection.

Materials Needed

One glove.

Procedure

Show your ungloved hand. Liken the hand to a spirit. Explain that when we lived in the premortal life with Heavenly Father, we were spirits. We could move (demonstrate with your hand) and think and spiritually grow.

Explain that we knew we could not be complete until we had gained a body, and so we chose to be born into mortality. At this point, put the glove on the hand. Help the class understand that the body houses the immortal spirit; the body moves, thinks, and grows because the spirit lives within the body. Because it is a mortal body, it feels physical pain.

Take off the glove and lay it down. Help the class understand that when we die the spirit leaves the body. The body no longer moves, but the spirit is still alive. The spirit still moves, thinks, and grows.

Put the glove back on the hand and explain that when we are resurrected, the spirit is reunited with the body. The body can move and think again because the spirit lives again within. However, the body is now perfect and will never separate from the spirit again.

Scripture Reference

2 Nephi 9:13.

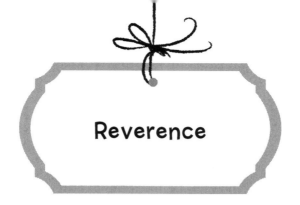

Reverence

Objective
To illustrate how small things can distract from the spirit of reverence.

Materials Needed
A small piece of thread.

Procedure
Prior to the lesson, place a piece of thread on the front of your shirt or jacket. It should be a color which will easily stand out on your clothing. Begin teaching a lesson on reverence. At an appropriate point, stop and ask if anyone noticed the thread. You will be surprised at the number of people who will respond. Ask enough questions to discover that a good portion of the class has been so distracted by the thread that they have paid little attention to the lesson.

Ask: If a small thread can keep us from listening in a meeting, how much more distracting is talking, text messaging, or any other form of inappropriate behavior or appearance? Our lack of reverence can distract others from concentrating, listening, or feeling the Spirit.

Scripture Reference
Doctrine and Covenants 84:54.

Sacrifice

Objective

To demonstrate that through sacrifice we gain an appreciation for our blessings.

Materials Needed

A glass of ice water.

Procedure

Display the glass of ice water and ask: Does this look good to you? Is it desirable? Most will express fairly positive feelings or interest in the water. Then ask them to imagine themselves in this situation: You have been working outside on a hot summer day. There is no shade, no breeze, and not a cloud in the sky. You have been mowing the lawn, digging holes for trees, or pulling weeds all afternoon. You are sweating and your mouth is dry from the dust. Ask: How desirable is the glass of ice water now, after this long day of hard work in the heat?

Explain that we experience a similar feeling in life when we sacrifice time, effort, or means for any good thing. This holy act of sacrifice leads us to a greater appreciation of what we have, even things which may seem simple or ordinary. Sacrifice helps us focus on our many blessings so often taken for granted.

Scripture Reference

Psalm 4:5.

Scriptures

Objective

To show that the scriptures can protect us if we use them.

Materials Needed

An umbrella and the scriptures.

Procedure

Hold up a closed umbrella and explain that it can protect us from the elements such as rain, sleet, or snow. Point out that it must be opened and used in order to offer that protection.

Liken the umbrella to the scriptures. The scriptures were given to teach us the truth, which protects us from Satan's deceptions and temptations. Remind the class that in order to protect us, the scriptures must be opened and used.

Scripture References

2 Timothy 3:16–17; Psalm 119:105.

Scripture Study

Objective

To show that how we study the scriptures makes a difference in what we gain from them.

Materials Needed

Two small pie pans, a rock, a sponge, and one cup of water.

Procedure

Put the rock in one pan and the sponge in the other. Ask: Which item will soak up more water? Pour half of the water over each item. Note that little or no water is visible in the pan with the sponge, but you can see nearly all the water in the pan with the rock. Ask: Why does one pan have more water than the other?

We are like the rock when we read our scriptures without purpose or focus; the truths of the scriptures run off and cannot fully penetrate our souls. We are like the sponge, however, when we prayerfully study the scriptures; we absorb gospel truths because the Spirit is able to teach us.

Scripture References

John 5:39; Mosiah 1:7.

Sealing Power

Objective

To illustrate one benefit of being sealed as a family.

Materials Needed

Two envelopes and two sets of individual pictures of family members. If pictures are unavailable, write the names on separate papers.

Preparation

Place a set of family pictures in each envelope. Leave one envelope open; seal the other.

Procedure

Hold up both envelopes. Explain that the open one represents a family who has not been sealed for eternity in the temple. The closed envelope represents a family that has been sealed. Point out that all families have problems during mortality. Give a few examples, such as poor health, marital strains, financial problems, busy schedules, and death. With each example, shake the two envelopes.

Soon the pictures from the open envelope will start to fall out, scattering onto the ground, illustrating that families who are not sealed can be separated by earthly problems. However, families who are sealed for eternity have more motivation and may receive strength to solve problems and remain together no matter what trial comes to them. They have the hope and promise of an eternal family if they live righteously and remain worthy to receive the blessings of being sealed.

Scripture Reference

Doctrine and Covenants 131:1–2.

Seeking the Good

Objective

To encourage us to seek for the good in everything.

Materials Needed

A jar with a lid, white rice, a coin, a key, a piece of hard candy, a marble, and a CTR ring. (Other small items can be substituted.)

Preparation

Fill the jar three-fourths full of rice. Add the small objects to the jar. Use a spoon to push them down into the rice so they are not visible from the outside of the jar. Place a lid on the jar.

Procedure

Display the jar of rice and mention that at first glance only rice appears to be in the container. However, if we search carefully, we will find more than rice. Post a list of the items that are also in the jar. Have a group member tilt the jar and move the rice to uncover each of the hidden items.

Compare this to our perspective in life. Often we must seek out and look for the best things in life, situations, or people. As a group, discuss blessings that may go unnoticed in our lives.

Scripture Reference

Articles of Faith 1:13.

Service

Objective

To illustrate how service to others lightens burdens.

Materials Needed

One large box filled with several heavy objects.

Procedure

Have a volunteer try to lift the box. (Ensure the volunteer does not get hurt.) Ask: Is it easy or difficult to lift the box? Is it heavy? Ask for two other people to help the first person lift the box. Together the task will be much easier.

Explain that the box and its contents are like the burdens we might experience in life. Discuss what some of these burdens might be. As members of the Church we have the responsibility to help each other. Offering service helps to lighten one another's loads.

Scripture Reference

Mosiah 18:8–10.

Spiritual Strength

Objective

To demonstrate how we achieve spiritual strength.

Materials Needed

A small hand weight.

Procedure

Show the weight to the group. Discuss the process of building muscles. Include in the discussion the importance of working out regularly, gradually lifting heavier weights, and doing more repetitions. Explain that over time, by doing these things, muscles will grow and strengthen. Brainstorm the benefits of physical strength.

Liken the process of building physical strength to the process of building spiritual strength. Ask: What must we do to strengthen our spiritual muscles? Answers might include scripture study, prayer, church attendance, fasting, service, and so on. Point out the need to develop our spiritual strength through faithful daily effort and continually striving to increase our obedience to gospel principles. Conclude by brainstorming the benefits of spiritual strength.

Scripture Reference

Ether 12:27.

Stewardship

Objective

To help us understand the meaning of stewardship.

Materials Needed

Any object that you greatly value, such as a piece of jewelry, a fishing pole, or a small electronic item.

Procedure

Show the item to the group. Explain why it is important to you. For example, mention who gave it to you or how long you saved money for it. Point out that if someone wanted to borrow it, you would only lend it to someone you trusted to be careful with it. If they were to misuse it, you would feel deeply hurt and disappointed in their careless behavior as a steward of something precious to you.

Likewise, when we came to earth, Heavenly Father trusted us to be wise stewards with this precious opportunity. We are his, and he cares deeply about us. To be careless with our time, talents, and general lifestyle hurts him. We need to be mindful of every action in order to show we are worthy stewards of that which belongs to our Father in Heaven.

Scripture Reference

Doctrine and Covenants 51:19.

Strengthening Family

Objective

To show that we, as individuals, can do much to strengthen our families in the gospel.

Materials Needed

Several large-sized children's blocks that lock or snap together.

Procedure

Display the blocks on the tabletop. Ask for suggestions of things one family member can do to strengthen the family (pray, smile, show respect, obey, etc.). Each time a new idea is suggested, put a block on top of or beside another. Do this until a wall begins to form. Ask: What would happen if we did at least one of these things for several days? Place an additional four or five blocks on the wall. Point out how much difference one person can make in strengthening the family. Liken the wall to a protection for the family.

Help the class members to understand that everything you have talked about also strengthens personal spirituality while strengthening the family. Similarly, as they continue to do things that increase personal spirituality, they also help protect family members. Discuss ways we can strengthen our personal testimony.

Scripture Reference

Doctrine and Covenants 88:122–23.

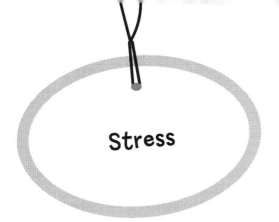

Stress

Objective

To illustrate the importance of reducing stress.

Materials Needed

A glass, water, and ice cubes.

Procedure

Fill the glass with water to the brim. Point out that even though the glass is completely full, you have not spilled any. State that if you are very careful, you can probably carry it around as you go throughout the day without spilling. Walk around the room, showing the full glass to each person, and then set it carefully on the table. Then pop a couple of ice cubes into the glass. The water will overflow.

Explain that our lives are like the glass of water. We often fill our lives to the brim with activities. As long as nothing unexpected happens we are fine. However, when anything unexpected comes into our already full lives (like the ice cubes), we can't cope with all of it. To reduce the stress and allow us to accomplish things in a positive manner, it is important to leave enough free time and resources to accommodate changes.

Scripture Reference

Mosiah 4:27.

Talents

Objective

To illustrate the value of individual talents.

Materials Needed

Sample pieces of several types of fabric. Select a wide variety of fabric, such as burlap, silk, denim, polyester, etc.

Procedure

Show the fabrics to the class and point out some of their differences. They look different and have varied uses. For instance, tell them burlap would be an excellent fabric for potato sacks. Silk is beautiful for formal wear, while denim makes great pants for work or casual wear. Each fabric is different, each has a special use, and each is important to us. This variety helps us meet various needs in life. A silk potato sack would not last very long, and a burlap prom dress would not be very comfortable.

Explain that as children of our Heavenly Father we are each different. Not only do we look different, but we each have different talents. All of these talents are important. Discuss what some of these different talents could be (compassion, painting, listening, speaking, etc.). Point out that one person's talents do not necessarily qualify him for another person's responsibility. We can share our own talents and draw on the talents of others to accomplish great things. We need all of the talents that our Heavenly Father has given to his children. All talents are different, but all have a special purpose, and all are important.

Scripture Reference

Doctrine and Covenants 82:18.

Temptation

Objective

To show how Satan uses temptation.

Materials Needed

Several brightly colored fishing lures.

Procedure

Show the fishing lures. Comment on how brightly colored and attractive they are. Introduce the purpose of using the lures: the bright colors, metallic shapes, and movements attract the fish. The ultimate purpose of the lure is to get the fish to strike at it. Help the class understand that when the fish strikes, the barbs are set and the fish cannot release itself.

Explain that Satan also uses brightly colored, appealing lures to attract us. Discuss what kinds of lures Satan might use. Be sure to identify why they would be considered a lure. Explain that the best protection we and the fish have is just to leave the lures alone.

Scripture References

1 Nephi 12:17; Moses 4:4.

Temptation

Objective

To illustrate that temptation can pull us off course.

Materials Needed

A compass and a small magnet.

Procedure

Demonstrate how the compass works. Explain that the needle always points to the magnetic north. Using the compass as a guide can keep you from getting lost and help you travel to your desired destination.

However, even the compass can be "pulled" from the right direction. Bring the magnet close to the compass; let the group observe how the needle is pulled away from pointing north, or off the right course. Point out that this is similar to one way Satan pulls us off the straight and narrow path. Discuss tools Satan could use to pull us in the wrong direction. Ideas might include peer pressure, media, and so on.

Note

This object lesson can be easily adapted to demonstrate Satan's deceptions by using a hidden magnet. Before class, place a magnet on a table and cover it with paper or a lightweight tablecloth. Display the compass to the group, and explain that the needle points to the magnetic north. Set the compass on the table and move it around in several directions to demonstrate that the needle continues to point north. Then slide the compass toward the magnet and allow the class members to observe the needle movement. (The needle will veer off toward the magnet.) Reveal the magnet and liken this to Satan's deceptions. Briefly discuss how deceptions can be hidden or appear harmless. If we're not careful, we might be pulled in the wrong direction, thinking we're still on course. We must be vigilant in order to discover his deceptions and see them for what they really are.

Scripture Reference
Alma 37:38–44.

Temptation

Objective

To demonstrate the importance of avoiding situations that can cause temptation.

Materials Needed

A magnet and a steel paper clip or a small steel washer.

Procedure

Place the magnet a short distance from the paper clip. Slowly bring the magnet closer to it. Point out how the paper clip begins to shake and then is quickly drawn to the magnet.

Liken this to placing ourselves in tempting situations. Although our intent may be to resist the temptation, if we allow ourselves to get too close to it, we can be pulled in quickly. To protect ourselves we must avoid tempting circumstances or remove ourselves if we perceive any danger.

Scripture Reference

1 Thessalonians 5:22.

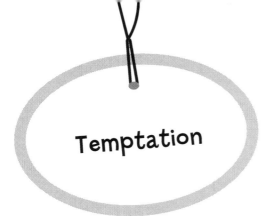

Temptation

Objective
To give insight to Satan's approaches.

Materials Needed
Water, red food coloring, red punch, and cups.

Preparation
Prepare two drinks: one made only of water and red food coloring and the other made of red punch.

Procedure
Begin with a discussion of Satan's enticements. Explain that he'll try hard to make his traps look appealing and good. However, true joy and happiness only comes from following our Father in Heaven. Anything else is only a counterfeit.

Follow this discussion by serving punch. Instead of punch, serve the drink made with food coloring and water. The class will notice the lack of flavor. Compare the drink to Satan's approach. He makes sin look so inviting; but once we partake, we realize it is a counterfeit to joy. Heavenly Father offers us the real thing—true joy. Conclude by serving the real punch.

Scripture References
Moses 4:4; Matthew 4:1–11.

Testimony

Objective

To demonstrate the importance of a personal testimony.

Materials Needed

Two people.

Procedure

Invite two people to stand in front of the group. Ask one person to lean against the other person whose feet are firmly planted. Ask: What would happen if the person with firm support moved? (The leaning person would fall down.)

Explain that our testimony is like the two people. At some points in life our testimony depends or leans on someone else's testimony (as children, new converts, and so on). However, a time may come when the person we lean against may not be available. It is important to gain our own testimony so that we no longer have to lean or rely on another's testimony. Discuss ways to develop a personal testimony.

Scripture References

Matthew 13:18–23; Alma 17:2.

Testimony

Objective

To help class members realize how our testimony can benefit others.

Materials Needed

A reflector.

Procedure

Display the reflector. Explain that it reflects light from another source and enables people who are in the dark to avoid danger and safely find their way. Emphasize that it does not make its own light; it reflects light from another source.

Explain that, in a sense, we are reflectors. Our light source is Jesus Christ, and we can reflect his love to other people through the testimonies that we live and bear. By reflecting the love of Christ, we can encourage others to keep away from the dangers of Satan's traps and help them find their way home to Heavenly Father.

Scripture Reference

Matthew 5:14–16.

Testimony

Objective

To encourage us to seek for a personal testimony.

Materials Needed

A bag and a mystery item to go into the bag (something easily recognized, but not too common).

Procedure

Before the lesson, place the mystery item in the bag, ensuring no one sees it. Invite someone to come up and feel what is in the bag. Instruct him or her to describe what it feels like—not what it is made of, only how it feels. (Example: It feels rough. It feels hard. It feels cold.) Allow three or four clues before the group tries to guess what it is. Usually they are unable to guess from just the description.

Next, invite another member from the group to feel the same object. Ask that person if he or she can tell what it is now. The second person should be able to easily identify the object. Emphasize that it is much easier to tell what something is by feeling it yourself than by having it described to you. As you feel the item for yourself you are more confident and certain of this knowledge.

Liken this to a testimony. Someone can describe his or her testimony to you, but to really know what a testimony is, you must feel it yourself. Once you feel it yourself, your doubts and uncertainties are removed. You will become confident in your own personal testimony of the truthfulness of the gospel of Jesus Christ.

Scripture Reference

Moroni 10:3–5.

Testimony

Objective
To illustrate that our testimony protects us.

Materials Needed
A small piece of bark from a tree.

Procedure
Display the bark. Briefly discuss the purpose of the bark on a tree. Point out that it protects the tree. If a tree loses too much bark, it can die from insects, exposure, and the loss of sap.

Explain that we have a similar protection in our spiritual lives. It is our testimony. A strong testimony can sustain us in times of turmoil. It can also keep us from giving in to temptations and doubt. Without a testimony we are more susceptible to the dangers of the world.

Scripture References
Helaman 5:12; Doctrine and Covenants 10:33.

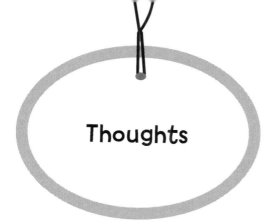

Thoughts

Objective

To show the value of virtuous thoughts.

Materials Needed

Two identical balloons, one filled with helium and the other with air. (Mylar balloons will hold helium much longer than latex balloons.)

Procedure

Hold one balloon in each hand. Discuss how the balloons are alike: size, color, shape, design, and so on. Tell the group that although they appear the same, they are different in one important way: one is filled with helium. Ask: How will that make a difference?

Explain that we are like the balloons because what we fill our minds with will determine whether we sink (drop the air-filled balloon) or soar (release the helium balloon). Discuss things we can do to promote virtuous thoughts.

Scripture Reference

Proverbs 23:7.

Thoughts

Objective

To show that our thoughts are influenced by what we are exposed to.

Materials Needed

Empty paper towel tube, several pieces of black paper crumpled into small balls, and several pieces of white paper crumpled into balls.

Procedure

Compare the paper towel tube to our minds. The things we put into our minds will affect our thoughts. Put a few black paper balls into the tube. Exposing our minds to inappropriate music, video games, images, movies, and other entertainment will lead to impure thoughts. Place several more balls into the tube as you list these influences until black balls begin to push out the other end.

Explain that in order to think good thoughts, we must seek after those things that are good and uplifting. Ask: What things might lead to good thoughts? As the class shares ideas, place white balls into the tube. Point out that it takes time to overcome the previous inappropriate thoughts, but eventually if we carefully select what we listen to, watch, and read, our thoughts will be wholesome. Continue placing white balls into the tube until they begin to push out the other end.

Scripture References

Doctrine and Covenants 88:118; 121:45.

Truth

Objective

To enable us to realize how vital the truth is to our lives.

Materials Needed

Two identical containers, bleach, water, and a plant.

Preparation

Put plain water in one container and water with one tablespoon of bleach in the other.

Procedure

Display the plant and place a container on each side of it. Tell the class that one container holds life-giving water for the plant and one holds poison that would kill it. Invite a class member to decide which container to use. Upon investigating, the person will easily detect the bleach by its strong smell.

Explain that in our lives we have a similar choice between two things: truth or lies. We must have the truth to guide our lives. If we are deceived, we may make decisions that jeopardize our eternal future. Satan and his deceptions are very clever. His counterfeits may appear to be good or true. We must be sure of the source before randomly accepting something as truth. This choice is as vital to our lives as it is to the life of the plant.

Scripture References

John 8:32; 14:6; Doctrine and Covenants 93:39.

Virtues

Objective

To show that our character can be enhanced by virtues.

Materials Needed

Two clear vases, liquid food coloring, and two fresh white carnations (or white irises).

Preparation

Fill one vase with water and several drops of food coloring. Clip off a small portion of the stem of one carnation (an angle cut is best) and place it in the vase. The tips of the carnation petals will take on the color of the food coloring.

Procedure

Show the untreated white carnation to the class. Discuss its beauty, and explain that our character is beautiful like the carnation. Clip the end and place it in the second vase filled with clear water. Put several drops of food coloring into the water.

Bring out the previously dyed carnation and observe how the food coloring has enhanced the beauty of the carnation, giving the petals a distinctive beauty. Liken the carnation to our character and the dye to positive traits and behaviors. Explain that these positive characteristics are sometimes called virtues. Discuss virtues that positively affect our character, such as gratitude, honesty, modesty, and patience.

Refer to the carnation that was placed in the water at the beginning of class. If it is fresh, it will have already begun to absorb the food coloring. Tell the class members that, like the dyed carnations, virtues can beautify and enhance our character.

Scripture References

Philippians 4:8; 2 Peter 1:5–8.

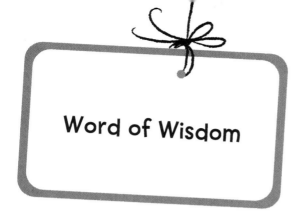

Word of Wisdom

Objective
To gain an understanding of the purpose of the Word of Wisdom.

Materials Needed
An owner's manual for a car.

Procedure
Show the manual and explain that the instructions are from the manufacturer. Give some examples from the manual, such as the type of oil to be used or the amount of air pressure for the tires. Point out that if these instructions are followed, the vehicle will most likely function properly and have a longer driving life.

Tell the class that Heavenly Father has given us a set of instructions for our bodies called the Word of Wisdom. When we follow his instructions, we are more likely to feel healthy, function better, and live longer.

Scripture Reference
Doctrine and Covenants 89.

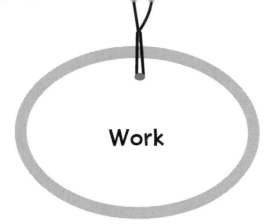

Work

Objective

To encourage us to seek Heavenly Father's help in our labors.

Materials Needed

An electric mixer or other small electrical appliance or tool.

Procedure

Display the mixer and discuss how it is used. Point out that in order for the mixer to accomplish what it was designed for, it needs to be plugged into a source of power.

Similarly, in order for us to accomplish all that we have been called to do, it is important that we are plugged into our source of power. We will achieve more and with much greater ease as we draw from Heavenly Father's unlimited power. With him we can accomplish marvelous things.

Scripture Reference

Philippians 4:13.

Worldly Influences

Objective

To demonstrate that we are influenced by our environment.

Materials Needed

A container of water.

Procedure

Display the water. Ask: What would happen if the water were put in the freezer? (It would turn to ice.) What would happen if it were heated on a stove? (It would boil.) Explain that the water is influenced by the atmosphere it is placed in.

Use this to illustrate that we are likewise influenced by the environment that we place ourselves in. Worldly influences will lead us into temptations and ultimately poor choices. On the other hand, good environments and activities will encourage Christlike behavior.

Scripture Reference

1 Thessalonians 5:21–22.

Worldly Pressure

Objective

To encourage us to live virtuous lives and resist worldly pressures.

Materials Needed

Sand, a cup, water, a fist-sized rock, and two pie pans.

Procedure

Just prior to the lesson, dampen sand and press it into the cup. Place the rock in one pie pan. Invert the cup with compressed sand into the other pan. Carefully remove the cup.

Begin by explaining that even a small amount of water can exert pressure and cause items to change. Demonstrate this by pouring water over the molded sand. Point out that some items are stronger and resist the pressure without changing. Pour water over the rock to illustrate.

Compare this to the pressure of the world to change us and our standards. Ask: How can we become strong enough to resist worldly pressures?

Scripture Reference

Helaman 5:12.

Young Men and Young Women Programs

Objective

To show that youth programs, including Duty to God and Personal Progress, work best when equally supported by the youth, the parents, and the leaders.

Materials Needed

A three-legged stool or table and three small signs to be attached with tape: youth, parents, leaders.

Procedure

Show the stool or table and ask: What would happen if one of the legs were missing? (The stool or table would fall.) What would happen if one of the legs were shorter than the other two? (It would be unstable.)

Explain that the stool is like the youth programs in the Church. To be effective and stable, youth, leaders, and parents must understand and be involved in the program. Attach the signs to each leg of the stool or table. Discuss what each of the three groups can do to help and support the others, including how each person will grow through their participation. Include suggestions for and benefits of working together on Personal Progress and Duty to God goals.

Scripture References

Doctrine and Covenants 107:99; see also Robert D. Hales, "Our Duty to God," *Ensign*, May 2010, 95–98.

SCRIPTURE INDEX

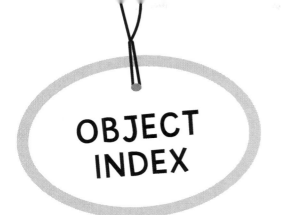

OBJECT INDEX

SUBJECT INDEX

ABOUT THE AUTHORS

Beth Lefgren and **Jennifer Jackson** have coauthored numerous books with a focus on teaching and providing leaders with creative ideas for presenting gospel lessons. They have offered leadership in the Primary, Young Women, and Relief Society organizations. Additionally, each has served on curriculum committees for The Church of Jesus Christ of Latter-day Saints and taught the Career Workshop at LDS Employment Centers.